A SLIGHT THING, HAPPINESS

SAINT JULIAN PRESS

POETRY

Also by Joan Baranow

In the Next Life
Blackberry Winter
Living Apart
Morning: Three Poems

Praise for A SLIGHT THING, HAPPINESS

In *A Slight Thing, Happiness,* Joan Baranow bears witness to things both slight and substantial with a linguistic lens that finds the beauty in all things: "White and rosy...ovaries / globular, like scrambled egg whites"; an embryo, "beautiful / waking like that / your moons urging you / to travel the edges of the dish"; an invalid grandmother "watching nothing but light / crawl along the walls"—and from a toddler son, "his voice, a few words warbling...*So beautiful,* he says, pointing / at the ordinary trees." Baranow celebrates "small things with or without wings," seeing them as the wonders that they are, with images that prowl and haunt this collection of syntactically acrobatic, passionately crafted poems.

— Terry Lucas

Poet Laureate Emeritus of Marin County, California

In her exquisitely rendered collection, *A Slight Thing, Happiness,* Joan Baranow tenderly maps the journey of becoming. Becoming a mother, becoming a family, becoming someone who understands what she would do "to bear a life." From the intricate intimacies of laparoscopic surgery to the strangely sensual seascape of a petri dish, Baranow's lush, incisive imagery reveals a scarred yet serene internal garden of organs and cells. From hospital beds to IVs and incubators, from the underdeveloped lungs of a preemie to the bruising love of early motherhood, these poems soothe and croon and bloom toward the messier, wilder garden that is the family and the world we live in. Yes, "the world flowers" in these poems, but never without acknowledgement of the work, care, and tending necessary to grow and survive through all of life's seasons, the labor of becoming. This is a vulnerable, honest, and truly beautiful book.

— Erin Rodoni

And If the Woods Carry You

Supreme among the values of poetry is its ability to delight, and that delight can take as many forms as poets can find. Among the delights of Joan Baranow's *A Slight Thing, Happiness*, there's the eye that gives us startling images ("wolves, their dense aromatic fur, / the red rash of their mouths"); or the ear that makes lizards "flit / like brisk secretaries." But there's also delight in this poet's engagement with the difficulties and triumphs of life and love; it is the kind of delight we all need, these days especially—the kind that brings hope.

— Robert Wrigley

A True Account of Myself as a Bird

A SLIGHT THING, HAPPINESS

Joan Baranow

SAINT JULIAN PRESS
HOUSTON

Published by
SAINT JULIAN PRESS, Inc.
2053 Cortlandt, Suite 200
Houston, Texas 77008

www.saintjulianpress.com

ISBN-13: 978-1-955194-08-2
ISBN: 1-955194-08-4
Library of Congress Control Number: 2022938257

Cover Art: *Murmurations*
Artist: ©Victoria Chaban

FOR THE FAMILY

CONTENTS

I

That Summer 3

Watching the Laparoscopy 4

In Glass 6

Toxemia of Pregnancy 8

After His Birth 10

Psyche 11

Surviving Miscarriage 14

Second Preemie 16

New Mother Again 18

Feeding the Son Born Premature 19

II

An Old Story 23

Grandma 24

The Visit 26

Sergeant Marge 28

Close Calls 29

Over the Phone 31

Diagnosis 32

Down a Sandy Road 33

You'd Like to Know 35

Inside Out 36

Settling 38

III

Things He Said   43
Discovery Museum   44
Beautiful   46
Heavy Rain   47
Bedtime   48
Five-Year-Old Waking   49
Elegy for Louise, our Cat   50
Negotiating with Nature   51
The Fawn   52

IV

Traveling Through   55
Disturbance   56
Chain of Being   58
Sanctuary   59
Hot Tub Conversation   61
Spring Births   63
At the Dance   65
Getting Reacquainted   66
Watching the Red Squirrels   68
Truckee River Rafting   69
Blue Moon   70

so much takes place on a clear day
old trees bearing plum and pear and apple

—Ann Pelletier, *Letter that Never*

A SLIGHT THING,
HAPPINESS

I

THAT SUMMER

Cobalt. Rust. A heave of fog
sliding across the sand.

Fog in the manzanita.

A flower like goldenrod put forth
its yellow pearls.
We posed nearby, where the wooden steps

left the parking lot.
The camera lens kept the edges in. Ocean. Cliffs.

A coastal summer. Before the baby
had being.
The seeds inside the shrubbery were neutral.

Coyote mint
whose scent drifted and disappeared.
Like foam. We stood on the deck

with a telescope's 25¢ view
of sunlit Pacific.
A boy leaping the trails.

I thought the same as anyone: the world flowers.
Even the lizard. Panting in the dust. Flowers.

WATCHING THE LAPAROSCOPY

You wouldn't guess how clean it looks –
white and rosy, the ovaries
globular, like scrambled egg whites,
the uterus dark and firm as a plum.
I could see now what they meant
in the medical texts, in those inadequate
drawings – only more lush, soft,
each organ self-contained. Strange,
I had imagined the gut was contiguous.
When the instruments entered in, the clamps
and probes, the pencil-like laser, I
did not feel sick, even when blood
pulsed from the split tubes, even
when he snipped them into petals
and crimped them back with a hot stick.
I wanted only to understand. My illness
had gone through the body thoroughly,
touching everything, and I had not known
how my own flesh had suffered, how it
sought to protect itself, without help.
And now scar tissue, thick, milky,
glimmers in the surgical light
like something poured from a basin,
a rich glue. When he slid the clamps
through my belly's incisions
they went straight down, they closed
like clam shells on the stuck organs.

We could see the adhesions then, shining
curtains under the hot blue flare,
before the laser split them
and the bowel fell back, the tubes
came loose, as if the surgeon
had snapped a puzzle apart.
I wanted to see it again, to know
where each piece of me went
after the surgery, how I would be whole,
but he fast-forwarded to the last
procedure – the Bruhat Technique –
and then the screen regained its blank blue.
I don't want to paint a rosy picture,
he said, *your chances are slim,*
and he used numbers and percentages
to prove I was as well as could be made.
Your eggs would've had to solve a maze
to get in. And now…
                    We got up to go.
I hope to hear some good news.
But already I saw the next surgery,
my children born in a sterile dish.
And now you ask what else I might do
to bear a life.

IN GLASS

Inside the glass   pearl & fish
a splash of blood

whereupon there came an explosion
bread rising   salt touching
the fragrant flour

O son   you were beautiful
waking like that
your moons urging you

to travel the edges of the dish

(pool of clear sand
reservoir of heat)

you must have liked
dividing

liked reaching into
the valleys of my womb

for when the others let go
when blood flooded my os
your heart would not stop

opening   closing

no lack of fire
leapt the synapses
of your brain

it was my flesh, failing
brought you forth

you took your first
teaspoon of air   and turned
dark rose

a hand on each foot

our world
gave you   gravity & a sky

TOXEMIA OF PREGNANCY

There was the bed bent in half,
the needle in the wrist,

the crack of bathroom light under the door.
Your father tried to sleep in the hospital cot

while the nurse came in every hour
to watch your heartbeat scratch itself

on ticker tape. Seven months inside me,
you must have liked the sugary IV

for never had you leapt so much
as if to say, OK, let me out.

I lay in a body whose cells had blown apart
and watched the clock move towards eight

when the surgeon would come lift you
feet first into air-conditioned light.

I tried to imagine how your world
would open onto this –

and even then I did not know
what "this" would be.

It was later, when you lay, breathing hard,
like an animal thrown by a car,

that I knew what I'd done to you,
though you were the "big boy"

among the mouse-sized children
who would also someday go home.

Each night after all day in the NICU
the imprint of alarm bells kept ringing

and I'd see that deep pit
in your chest gasping fast. On the third day

when I first held you
you seemed a little surprised

and you slept in the fragrance of my skin.
Little one, sweetest pea, I crooned,

too new for mothering to sing
any of the songs I had rehearsed.

How we all love beginnings best,
and there you were, learning to breathe.

AFTER HIS BIRTH

That bowl of iris and orchids on the bedside table.
A purple blur. Green fragrance.

Then the doctor's sneakers under the plastic curtain.
Assurances from the Prussian General. His hand
On the blanket on my institutional knee.

My husband sometimes here. Sometimes with our son.

Springtime was a bank of unborn acacias.
Before the yellow whiff. Inside the hospital

I heard the corridors hush us to sleep.
Spinal Block. Mom Sleeping.

He slept while working hard.
Each breath a pinch in his chest
Thirty miles away in his isolette.

Under the heat lamp. Conscious.

When he came back he said our son knew his voice.
Stopped breathing five, six times.

Too noisy in the NICU to read.
I could smell exhaustion in his shirt.

Imagined nothing.

The phone kept ringing instead.
The nice nurse. The smart nurse. The thin nurse

With the cartoon stethoscope. Next –
Learning how to sit up. To eat.

Fear crouched on the quiet carpet.
We kept the fan on for company.

I liked the orange slices, the cottage cheese.
My husband coming in with no bad news.

Oxygen needs falling. No intubation.
Insurance said I could have three nights in the sterile sheets.

But I said the magnesium had to go.
I said I'd leave on Sunday.

By four o'clock the rain had stopped. Stargazers. Daisies.
A crowd of freesias. We trundled outdoors in the wheeled
    cart.

The land we drove over had softened somewhat. Become
    gentle.
His just being here had done that.

PSYCHE

After weeks hauling her heavy belly
from task to task, helped by armies

of ants, slippery reeds, an eagle's talons —
after she'd crawled into the earth,

the coin in her mouth,
bread in her hand,

and seen the Queen of Death seated
among the lush rot —

after she'd taken the token gift
and climbed back into the strange day,

feeling the first worried pangs
of female labor —

she'd had enough.
Enough of being jerked around.

Whatever was in that bejeweled box
belonged to her, whatever the cost.

The sleep that came? What of it?
Rest was what she needed,

a mortal sleep
to keep her unborn daughter safe

and herself secure. Let sleep
anchor her to the plush earth,

let the rock-strewn moon
hover over. Soon enough she'll wake

thrashing in a sheet of sweat
to what the Goddess had tried, and failed, to terminate –

SURVIVING MISCARRIAGE

for Duston

At six weeks you held on
even as your companions
let go the little notches they'd made –
like rock climbers on a slippery cliff
they stuck their crampons into ice,
breathing the liquid air, despairing
even as the face of the wall
gave way, and they fell
down the path they'd come,
an avalanche of blood behind them.
You tightened your grip,
your cells, even then, knowing
what it took,
the blood you wouldn't need
sliding past. The cramps
lasted an hour or so,
and then we could hear your heart again
inside the emptier space.
Now the stars belonged only to you,
the woman in whose womb you slept
entirely yours.
They had climbed nearly to the summit,
your fraternal twins,
they had traveled without words,
crippled in ways we'll never know.

While we waited safely at sea level,
you buried yourself stubbornly
against the precipice,
your yolk sac intact, everything
for the journey secured.

SECOND PREEMIE

Sleepless, I hauled my hugeness
to the side of the bed,
hooked the wheelchair with my foot
and leaned into it, shuffling
forward a few steps at a time
down the long hallways to the NICU
where you slept in your isolette,
bunched up, like a baguette
warm under the heat lamp,
your face obscured by the CPAP,
wires fixed to your veins.
You seemed content,
covered with pre-term fur
and a diaper sized for a doll.

The nurse asked if I would like to hold you,
I did not, I wished only to gaze,
to let you sleep in your fetal dream,
but she pulled you out anyway,
looping tubes through the portals
to lay you, light as a loaf of bread,
into my arms. Up close
I saw your pinched face,
one eye smaller than the other,
your skin the color of walnut
and wrinkled like one, tiny creases
worrying your forehead.

I feared I might drop you
for lightness, a cloth napkin
slipped from my lap.
And then your eyelids fluttered,
and your mouth crumpled
into weak, fierce cries.

Please, I said, put him back,
so she slid you onto the tray,
adjusted the CPAP, and you curled up
and calmed yourself from within.
I sat in the room with its muffled
bleats and shrieks, watching you sleep
while my milk came in.
All you had to do was breathe
and that was enough.

NEW MOTHER AGAIN

Traffic disperses
and the empty lot lets the wind
simmer. Your four-year-old
scribbles an alternating current.
You keep sneaking peeks at your infant's
hairy, adorable face, the surprise
of his eyes landing on yours.
Yet you'd give anything to sit an hour
in sulphur water, among strangers,
hearing the piped mineral spring
fall from tub to tub, cooling.
Even folded up in coach fare
would give you an essential respite.
You'd like that, leaning against the cold
window, a plastic cup of Coke
on a tray. From there you'd watch
suitcases roll like small cars being towed
to tropical destinations.

FEEDING THE SON BORN PREMATURE

I stir rice in the pot,
put some on a plate,
and think, as always, of the story
about the starving Chinese family
in which the father chewed the few
grains left, then put them
into his baby's mouth.
I tell my son, "It's good, good,"
and move his hand to the fork,
his solid 2-year weight on my lap.
When he first came home,
he hadn't yet made his brown fat,
his chest was creased
like a vase cracked and glued back again.
For six months I kept watch
for another apneic lapse
like the one as he lay in the NICU
when his father and I cooed to him
and he stopped his breath
to listen hard, and then forgot
to breathe again.
I fell faint to the chair as the electronic
bells kept bleating
until a nurse gave him a casual pat.
Once when home he slept so deeply
I couldn't wake him
and shook him the way I shouldn't,
shouting his urgent name
until he opened his aggrieved eyes.

And so I watch, as I must,
as he eats the gold rice
glazed with fat, make sure he has
as much as he wants.

II

AN OLD STORY

Her heart was larger than I'd thought,
leaking from the burlap sack
he brought back to me,
flabby even, laced with veins.
I'd expected a dainty tidbit,
something fit for a canapé,
a sip of wine,
not this slab of purple meat
pulsing on the plate.
I ordered the fire lit, candles,
a goblet, my best brocade, servants
to observe her final disposition:
her disappearance down my throat.
I had my huntsman mince the dish,
drizzle honeyed sauce over it.
Each piece tough and delicious,
her body entered mine.
Yet when I went to my mirror,
my beloved double, I saw
no beauty but the curse
of motherhood mocking me,
the same sorry face
shattering the glass.

GRANDMA

She dreams of wolves, their dense aromatic fur,
the red rash of their mouths. Daylong,
she lies there, the woven covers drawn tight
to her chin, watching nothing but light
crawl along the walls.
Once, she had carried an axe.
Once, she had flayed the little doves
so plentiful here, the specks of their eyes
bright onyx gems. She'd chewed their tough
sinews, boiled their bones.
She washed, put up peppers, swept
the oiled boards, kept all her needles
in a cushioned box. Now
she lies still with sickness,
the stink of her sweat like a dump.
And that weakling of a girl – miniature
of her mother – creeping in,
her cloak puddled on the floor,
jabbing a spoon of tepid tea to her lips.
Ghastly. But she's the ghost now, isn't she,
blasted, blown, her legs like twisted rags,
her stomach a pale pit. *Get up!*
her dream voice shouts. In dreams
she crowbars the bloated door and goes
past the cracked lintel, her whole heft erect,

no one's lullaby. Out there
is where she finds them
encircling the house, her own
rough pack sniffing the land,
ears turned to the woman who's had enough –
frail, naked, old.
She takes a step, holds out her hand.

THE VISIT

I see the window's unlatched again.
The philodendron she gave me
is glum. The dream I'd been saving,
what was it? – moths
masquerading as lacy lingerie,
my mother spitting molars
into a drum – slips
from beneath my lids
and dissolves into the room's
dank breath.
She comes in then, unfolding
the compartments of her basket:
bread, butter, a plastic knife
(she still won't trust me
after that last pathetic swipe),
jars of jam inked in her mother's
loopy hand. Her red wool hat
is steamy. Rain?
Once again she fools me.
She's her daddy's daughter: small
tense fingers quick to tie things up.
I like the way she's whittled
her nose into new angles.
I'd eat if I could remember how.
And it's difficult when the sheet
tucks so tightly under my chin.
It's been weeks since I saw my feet
though I trust they're there,
faithful as spring allergies.

She smears a torn piece of bread
and bites. Hungry, yes.
She's tramped through three miles
of woods, past
what I can't forget:
salamanders, lady slippers, quail,
past the ghost wolf rumored to haunt
the hydrangeas outside my house.
I'd be on my own but for her
mercy visits.
On days when light strikes the ceiling
I watch the spiders spin.
Oh, if you could see my garden!
Foxglove, primrose, dahlias
lush as strawberry cream.
The year the peonies came back,
I touched his rough fur.
But that's as far away as a dream.
They hung his body from a myrtle branch.
Come on, Grandma, wake up, she says. Eat.

SERGEANT MARGE

She strained against the hospital bed,
her wrists knotted to the metal rail,
her hair frayed, her eyes
black stones, her nose as fierce
as her broken nails.
My husband in his white coat was coaxing her,
Come on, Marge…
Her arms kept jerking against the ties,
finding the length of her leash –
I won't go back there, she snapped.
But even I, quiet by the door,
who'd never seen anyone tied
to a bed before, knew the facts.
They'd found her at home, covered with shit.
The social worker clutched the clipboard
to her chest, grim, capable,
confident as a lamppost.
Fifty years in the army, Marge
thinks she can win this one too.
But in this war only the documents win.
Look at the words typed in their correct spaces.
Look at the dotted line.

CLOSE CALLS

Therefore I will not keep silent;
I will speak out in the anguish of my spirit,
I will complain in the bitterness of my soul.
                                                 Job 7:11

Our mid-morning nap, my five-month-old
like a folded blanket on my chest,
when the phone ringing startles me up
and my sleeping son flips to the floor
face down on the flokati rug.
I lift him like a drowning child,
a burning boy from the flames.
Unbruised, he doesn't even cry.

Or the time I was chatting at the poolside party,
turned away from my four-year-old
afloat on the sturdy plastic raft,
it was just for a minute, believe me,
how did I know he'd step off, bored as he was,
reaching for the wall, water closing over his head,
that an older boy would see him sink,
jump in and rescue him?

Close calls, the fractions of accidents,
the young man brushing broken
windshield glass from his jacket,
the surgeon who nearly nicks the femoral nerve,

even I, seven months gone, days away from seizure,
saved by the OB who said, "It's time
to get that baby out." Close calls.

What are they but rehearsals for the real thing?
Under the rush of gratitude,
of falling to our shaking knees,
we know – there will be a next time
without reprieve or rescue, the cancer
will split its capsule, the driver won't swerve.
On that day prayers are dust in your mouth.
You'll remember Job's wife, curled weeping
on a frayed rug in a corner of that cursed room.

OVER THE PHONE

I could hear a cloud
in your voice, mom,
through the telephone's static.
You said it was *nothing, just*
not having enough to do,
like an old lady,
and how you caught yourself
walking stooped over into the post office
and thought *I don't need*
to walk like that.
It's not the needles you fear,
I know that.
It's the memory of your own mother
in bed, unable to get up,
to feed or to wipe herself.
It's having to ask anything of us.

DIAGNOSIS

There was no extra cervix to give her,
no spare vagina, no bladder,
she was punctured from inside,
tumors escalating
like pent gasses through O-rings,
organs exploding under the skin.

NASA had been warned – likewise,
radiologists sent their reports.
But for the sake of a great day, blue skies,
television crews already assembled,
what's a degree or two
when everyone's suited up,
ready to launch? She needed no scan,
stretched there on the table,
a stranger's fingers palpating her inoperable tumor.

Nothing to do but drive home
and make the terrible calls.

DOWN A SANDY ROAD

The light in the little cemetery
was liquid lead
glazing the scene, hardening.

Someone snaps a picture
of brothers who practice
speaking to each other.

Baked beans and potato salad,
cold chicken.
A basket of plastic forks.

The talkative realtor
your mother never liked
gives you her card.

Three loads of her life
in a borrowed flatbed
to the dump.

What to do with her ceramic frogs,
jeans she had patched
with hands that taught you to sew?

Emptied and sold,
buried
and left behind.

Maybe I should have stayed
to watch the crew of local boys
lower her in.

YOU'D LIKE TO KNOW

We were all there,
bereaved and bewildered,

fumbling the forms of ritual —
a poem, an aria, a picture

and flowers balanced on the box
that held you hovering

over the draped hole.
The winter sun was there,

the ground brittle with pine.
We kept sighing, resigned.

INSIDE OUT

I think of your bones dismantled in the sodden box,
your flesh completely eaten, dissolved, an apparatus

not you but just a sketch of human form,
so now I can imagine you as you were before, in life, intact,

wading the warm sandbars with grandkids at the Cape
or holding our dying cat on your lap, combing his matted fur.

While you were still in denial we drove to the marina
where you fancied a houseboat family reunion next year

beyond when would be – what was – your death.
You drove the clunky van, pointing out the rolled down
    window,

for by then the tumor had wasted your strength, it was hard
    to walk,
though you pretended health for my sake.

I think of weeks wasted at a stretch not calling you,
wishing you would call. Too late to know that's not

how I should have loved you. Too late to know
this poem is useless undeliverable.

You preferred cheap tennis shoes, weak black coffee, plastic
    dishware,
you went into the world at sixteen

to be married, to be a mother, defying your mother
with simple hopes that none of these facts can evince,

your imprint on the earth so slight, so easily wiped away
a handheld brush could do it, no matter what I scrawl.

None of us was there to assist your passing from one world
to the next, as you had done for us in your young glory.

Even now I can hear you scoff at *glory*. Joan, you said,
it happens *to* you, like being turned inside out.

Is that what it's like? What life does to us, forcing us
    to unfold?
Grieving, bereft, we're left on this earth to watch

as mothers pass from speech unto death,
too late for last words, words like unsent letters clasped
    to the chest.

SETTLING

This is just the kind of cheap box I asked for
years before my diagnosis.
Not the plane crash I half joked about being
the best way to die, but close enough.
I see you chose something nice from my closet.
I appreciate that. I just wish I'd – well –
being buried here? Not ideal, but
I'd never have chosen among you children.
What's it matter anyway? I'm gone.

It's a quiet place. That's what I liked
about this backwater village.
I could sit on the roof of my house
and smoke. If only Louise hadn't published
a prayer for me in the local paper
I could have died without embarrassment.
No one does, I guess. I mean the shame
of lying there, stiff. Of being discovered.
Of being undressed and washed or whatever
it is they do to you before closing the lid.

I'm sorry it happened the way it did.
But I'm okay. The pine tree you picked
to bury me under drops its needles
in winter like a blanket. That's an image
meant to tell you I'm tucked in
even though the cold can't touch me.
There, there, my Sweet Petunia,
you were always too sensitive.

Listen, if it helps to know,
I'm scattered down here the way I like.
See how the scrub grass grows
so reliably over my grave.

III

THINGS HE SAID

for Gabriel

He said he'd run out of dream power.
He'd see if I had any extra.
He wanted to floor his room with sod
to plant bamboo
and why couldn't he spread sod on the floor?

He said he and his friends gathered together
in a little herd.
He said if you get hurt I'll kill you.
He said call me Black Eye.
He said when Frankenstein was first made
he was a jolly soul.

When his father said to watch out for those
Paris Hilton types,
he said, So you have some experience with that?

He said call me Inside the Rainbow.

DISCOVERY MUSEUM

Built into a fake, rubbery tunnel under the bay,
one pint-sized aquarium

where a neon plastic crab captures
the children's greedy attention.

I crouch down and peer through smeared glass
at two fish: one upright, mouthing the surface,

the other nosing close to an actual crab,
mud-colored, escutcheon-shaped, its spidery legs

covered with a mossy algae resembling bread mold.
Hooked to its rock, it reaches toward a bright

tangerine starfish, and with sharp precision
plucks a thin strip from its arm,

which was already slit
and folded back, revealing white flesh

like the weak underside of a woman's arm.
The crab stuffs the strip into its mouth –

a hidden, busy, orifice –
and reaches again, while

children swarm the room,
each world oblivious:

the crab shredding its prey,
the children as they shriek and play.

BEAUTIFUL

At the pet store: no rabbits.
But plenty of mice, spinning
inside what my son calls
Ferris wheels. He strokes the glass

cages and feels fur,
the trembling of miniature hearts.
Next: fish. Here too he swipes
the smooth aquariums, sees

goldfish back off. *Mommy,*
sit right here, he orders,
smacking the floor, then snags
another pretzel from his bag.

An indoor outing today, the sky iffy,
Richardson Bay so gray
it looks smeared with dirt.
This morning, raking leaves, I hear

his voice, a few words warbling.
What? I ask, shoving the leaves.
So beautiful, he says, pointing
at the ordinary trees. Beautiful.

HEAVY RAIN

Yesterday we saw
a stiff rat in a rivering gutter,
its death so public,
the cold, pink paws caught begging.
I had my son on my back,
climbing the water-sluiced staircase
behind the church up to the road
where our house stood.

I tried to look with a poet's love
of the elements –
waterlogged hills,
trees sinking under bloated
folds of water, my street strewn
with strips of eucalyptus –
and thought how only the young
can love the eye's transparency,
Emerson's extravagance,
a wish to dissolve
into anything other –

anything other
than a rat tumbling against gravel,
asphalt bruising its back,
its belly's fur blurred with rain.

BEDTIME

The time glows green. The fan's
wind shifts the curtains. Our son

comes in, touches the bed.
"I don't know if I've been asleep

or awake." He crawls in,
his slim body like a pencil lead.

I lie here, unable to find
my drift of dream, recalling

homework heavy on his desk,
the clock's energy and fatigue,

a teacher's anxious cheer:
"Maybe you shouldn't make it negotiable."

Discipline. Handwriting. Addition.
The day's divisions.

FIVE-YEAR-OLD WAKING

Today, he does not order me back
into my room. Instead, he
opens one of his large eyes
and asks, "What, Mom?" and I say,
"I love you," softly, he is awakening
for school this morning, a catechism
in disappointment. He dips his face down
into his sheets, sighs, tucks
his arms under his chest. 8:00.
I am adding up the minutes for breakfast,
getting dressed, morning pee, knowing
how it is to rise slowly from sleep,
scarves of dreams drifting.
He is wearing blue pajamas with WWII
planes imprinted on clouds.
He believes he will live forever
in this house, that wherever I go,
he will go, too.
I stand by the bedside, waiting,
as he pushes the blanket back
and sits up, resistance
slipping from his shoulders,
an admiral accepting peace.
He says, "OK, Mom,"
and gets out of bed in mild obedience.

ELEGY FOR LOUISE, OUR CAT

She lay on a borrowed blanket, her leg wrapped
with green tape, readied for the catheter.
Starved by illness, her skin a jaundiced gold
where she'd been shaved a week ago –
still, her fur was fragrant, her desires intact.
She pushed against me, wanting down from there,
then let us stroke her knobby back.

We spoke of rare mutations, her vet and I,
how the virus had spread inside the gut,
attacked the marrow bone, and no one
and nothing knew how to stop it.
The end was quick. Twenty seconds? Ten?
He pressed the scope against her heart.
Stopped, he said. And found a sheet to fold her in.

At home I gentled her into a box,
smoothed the dug earth over her.
What else? Just a spray of hyacinth
to mark the grief I can't bring myself to speak.

NEGOTIATING WITH NATURE

I'd show him the newts
shiny as licorice,
hiding under the heavy planters,

but he runs to my lap,
afraid of insects and salamanders,
small things with or without wings,

though he can slide down a curved tube
five times his size,
or walk atop a stone wall, pigeon-toed,

watering the Persian lilies.
I'd like to help him touch a snake,
feel the slick mother-of-pearl scales,

let the snake tongue taste his palm.
When summer heat comes
we could look for lizards along the trail

and watch them flit
like brisk secretaries.
Casualness, they say, is the best

virtue of mothering.
I'll have to set the rock back
and step aside.

THE FAWN

She lay in the bay laurel debris,
her neck thrown back,
her hooves pressed together
like fingertips in prayer.

There had been two of them.
My son liked to watch the fawns
from the window
and would slap the window glass
to make them look up.

At first, we couldn't tell
what the doe was doing, licking
them so much, until the flesh
around their necks sloughed
and then just disappeared.

I suppose she knew something of disease
and had only this one remedy.

My son leaned towards the still fawn,
not knowing what death is yet,
and I touched the arm of the stranger
who had come to trim my trees.
Look, I said, Oh, look.
and we stood there while I tried to tell
the story of her life.

IV

TRAVELING THROUGH

From the frosted car window
I saw a single reed, wet, snow-blown,
half broken, sticking up from dead roots
in a fallow land between fields
where a narrow creek thaw
etched a black scar against the snow.

Already past now, the wheels of my rented car
skidding a little, I remembered how
my teenage tennis shoes would slide
sideways, soaked, as I walked
nowhere across the muddy hillocks.
Back then my soul had a chance to travel
where the land was useless –
just fields of abandoned apple trees,
a chickadee gripping a stiff twig,
a dull gray sky and tractors gouging
diagonal rows into the low hills.

I felt my soul yearn
for such stunned poverty.
Even so, I did not stop the car
to walk, as I wished, through the sloshy decay.
Something else was taking me toward – or from –
and I did not know if I would return.

DISTURBANCE

I heard the scurry
of urgency, animals
knocking wood out back,
stacked lumber falling.

I got up without my slippers,
went to the door,
flicked the backyard light, saw

two coyotes – dog-like,
raccoon-like, fox-like,
reddish, dense, plush,

the alpha on high ground, tail straight,
the meek one a few feet below,
tailed tucked tight,

his stance sideways,
the stance of a man begging

and he was,

the sounds from his throat
guttural,
muttering *no* over and over,
having already given in.

The alpha stood stiff
then lunged,

tumbling downslope,
twisting deep in the weeds,
crushing them,

then suddenly apart.

Again and again the same
stance   silence   cowering cough.

My camera's flash
lifted the alpha's face,
flat, incurious, noting me in my robe,

his gaze a blank page

before he drove the other
further into the dark

dry hillside
of the neighbor's yard.

CHAIN OF BEING

Years ago
in the South, pulling wood chunks
from a vine-strangled stack,
I let a flock of termites loose.

They flew upwards
on white, moth-like wings,
ghost insects,
and then without warning

dragonflies snatched them,
swooping in
like chunky bombers.

Where had they been hiding?
Or not hiding
on bark or leaf, invisible
to blunt eyes.

I know so little about
what I love.

SANCTUARY

for my mother

You chose a place hard to get to – 23 miles to the gulf from
Old Town, past longleaf pines and wiregrass marsh. We took
the interstate from Orlando together, stopping for biscuits

and grits at a southern kitchen along the way. Halfway to
Suwannee, on the country highway flanked by solid woods,
we gasped at a panther dashing straight across.

I must have been on grad school break – you were only 48.

Two rooms and a bathroom up on stilts. A hot pot for
coffee. Years later I found you a little fridge. Back then it was
snacks from the package store, an evening out at Salt Creek
restaurant that would gladly fry a day's catch. You talked of
building a dock, of getting a little boat.

Your neighbor Louise, wiry and tough, was enough of a loner
to suit you.

Such an alien place with skittery palmetto bugs under the
garbage bin. Spanish moss snagged on bald cypress, crepe
myrtle, cabbage palms, your own curve of canal, a single
banana tree. Rattlesnakes and cottonmouths. Magnolia
blossoms like white doves nested among rusty leaves.

The heat smelled sweet.

You'd climb to the roof for a view and a smoke, take photos of five turtles sunning on a fallen log slanted into the canal. Enough to keep you driving back and forth from Ohio with the cats until you retired, by then too late to enjoy it much.

You believed people were made for happiness. My last visit there, you kept your cheer despite the growth, undiagnosed. After you died, we found Christmas gifts still wrapped among the clutter.

I've stopped yearning for a heavenly reunion. There are days when I don't even think of you. On this opposite coast I look from a window into an overgrown plum tree reaching into an oak.

The oak arches, holds to the earth.

HOT TUB CONVERSATION

When I call you at college you're on your way
to the farmer's market, hoping the tamale stand
is still open, or you're practicing chords
to Tárrega's *Lágrima,* liking how tough it is,
or you're at a thrift store picking out
a gift for us, an idyllic
village scene to put on a shelf.

These days I let myself believe happiness
has snuck back after years of flirting
with someone else's lovely son, while mine
suffered through drab years
at the school of "pods" next to
the sewer plant. In winter, you said,
the parking lot would flood and once a car
backed into the utility pole
and the lights went out. How bitter
it felt to be kept in the dark with wet shoes,
everyone's middle school angst on display.
I knew so little about you, hurrying
from work to the rec center pick-up,
hurrying you home for homework.

Not until that December night
in the Sierras, your senior year,
our motel room surrounded by snow,
the stairs to the outdoor hot tub
iced over, you ran in your boots and towel,

I gripped the frozen rail, and together
we slipped into the heat, and there
you told me you'd finally forgiven
yourself and stopped caring too much,
that you'd been a bad friend
to your friends and were ready
to feel okay again. You, my paragon
of cortesia, my patient one. The steam
lifted and dispersed, the sky
was deep black above us where stars
kept their course. I said something
you shrugged off, delicately,
and then a couple came shivering
out of their room to plunk themselves
into our sanctum,
so we got out and went back
to our room where your father
waited with his happy grin.

SPRING BIRTHS
for Rick

Tonight the new moon
looks like the rim of an eyelid.

Wisteria winds around the redwood porch.
Orange blossoms open.

It's May, and again your birthday
returns,
a fortieth fanfare this year.

Surprising, isn't it, that nothing hurts,
that instead you've reaped tenfold
from the seeds you'd sown.

Iris, daisies, forget-me-nots,
wild white onion,
a new blue star-shaped Lithadora
the deer might eat,
all the flowers I can see from here

and more yet to come,
a bag of bulbs in the shed.

To think you were born
in the rush of cherry blossoms.

What luck that Congress
would add an extra hour of light to your day.

So let this fax machine
send blessings
and love from afar, Maychild,

poet, father, friend,

forty years circling a star.

AT THE DANCE
for Huynh

She wears what might have been
her country's flag, a flowing sari,
or blankets stolen from the cavalcade.
She might have wrapped an infant
in soft folds and carried him
from the jungle thick with napalm
onto the dawn-launched boats,
her own hair burning.
On this dance floor crowded
with the devourers of milk and honey,
she sways delicately,
pleased with the disco throbbing,
the strobe-lit ceiling.
If the divine exists, as it must,
here it would be, in her
whose mother was found floating
face down on the Yellow River,
the mother she hated.
She swings the scarf
that hangs from one shoulder,
gathers her hair grown back,
and dances with us.

GETTING REACQUAINTED

First, lift the little flap
of hair over my left ear
and croon an old tune –
Froggy Went a-Courtin'
or *The Girls of Brighton Beach*.
Let your ticklish lips
push vowels into the tunnel
where my tiny bones tremble.
Fashion my favorite tonic
of pomegranate fizz
then hold both my heels
while reciting a recipe for trouble.
Conjure thunderclouds.
A well-timed slice of lightning
has never failed to fling
off my clothes.
You, however, must keep
wearing that absurd
orange plaid vest
with buttons of bone.
It reminds me
of all your daughters
and their ten pregnancies.
Your huge female clan
and goofy smile
has certainly undone *me*.

So while we're here
in this heavy four-poster,
rain like horse hooves
charging the skylight,
remember the silly
delights we've never put words to.
Tell me I'm a koi
and you're the stream
I swim in,
golden bronze
in the garden pond
like a fat calico cat.

WATCHING THE RED SQUIRRELS

We sat in the kind of heat
the aged seek, three electric
heaters burning at our feet

while outside the sun blazed
the squirrel's strawberry tail.
One leg with its delicate foot

stuck straight up,
like a child reaching too far
into a bucket

only to tip
and flip inside
the cracked plastic feeder

hanging by its chain.
Your mother and aunt laughed.
So did we.

It was one of those afternoons
that remains in memory.
A slight thing, happiness.

TRUCKEE RIVER RAFTING

The least heart leaps at the sight
of these giddy boats bouncing downstream,
a carnival caravan carrying crews of Speedo-
thonged and bikini-clad beauties,
the season's image of summer's innocence.
Go then, unlace your tennis shoes,
wade through shallows – your toes
have never felt so exquisitely cold –
and slip belly-first into a buoyant dinghy.
Someone will surely hoist you up,
offer you a beer. You'll feel the snag
and shudder as the raft regains its glide
and the shore with its sullen chores
retreats. Now the sun unleashes
its heat, the river flexes its muscles.
As the boat begins to spin
between banks of sage and sunflower,
a girl with a Gibran tattoo
inked lavishly across her chest –
For Love is Sufficient unto Love –
invites you to steer
through the afternoon's eternal blue.

BLUE MOON

The moon lingers below the horizon
sending a sheen up in advance
like an envoy shouting the queen's arrival

only the moon's just a bony
crone, like me, hooked to the earth
by the same threads – and yet

here I am in the car, watching
its curved rim crowning
over the ridge and

sliding without effort into the sky.

ACKNOWLEDGMENTS

I am grateful to the editors of the magazines and anthologies in which the following poems appeared:

The Breath of Parted Lips: "Beautiful"

Carquinez Poetry Review: "The Visit"

The Gettysburg Review: "Grandma"

Pulse – Voices from the Heart of Medicine: "Toxemia of Pregnancy"

Spillway: "Getting Reacquainted"

Tell Me Again – Poems of Illness and Healing: "You'd Like to Know"

The Western Humanities Review and *Stories of Illness and Healing: Women Write Their Bodies* (reprint): "Watching the Laparoscopy"

The Yalobusha Review: "In Glass"

"That Summer," "Watching the Laparoscopy," and "In Glass" were published in the chapbook *Blackberry Winter* (Talent House Press).

Special thanks to artist Victoria Chaban, and her marvelous artwork *Murmurations*, a detail of which appears on the front cover. *Website: https://www.victoriachabandesign.com*

Thanks and deep appreciation to my publisher, Ron Starbuck, for his dedication to poetry and his eye for beautiful book design.

And, as ever, gratitude and love to my family, to my Ensenada poet buddies, and especially to Ann.

ABOUT THE AUTHOR

Joan Baranow is the author of *In the Next Life*, *Living Apart*, and two poetry chapbooks. Her collection, *Reading Szymborska in a Time of Plague*, won the 2021 Brick Road Poetry Book Contest. A fellow of the Virginia Center for the Creative Arts and member of the Community of Writers, she founded and teaches in the Low-Residency MFA program in Creative Writing at Dominican University of CA. With her husband David Watts she produced the PBS documentary *Healing Words: Poetry & Medicine*. Her feature-length documentary, *The Time We Have*, presents an intimate portrait of a teenager facing terminal illness.

www.ingramcontent.com/pod-product-compliance
Lightning Source LLC
Chambersburg PA
CBHW020212090426
42734CB00008B/1032